T0083344

Fiddle Time Sprinters

Violin accompaniment book

Kathy and David Blackwell

Teacher's note

These duet parts are written to accompany the tunes in *Fiddle Time Sprinters*. They are an alternative to the piano accompaniments or CD, and are not designed to be used with those items.

We are grateful to Simon Stace for all his help in road-testing these duets.

Kathy and David Blackwell

MUSIC DEPARTMENT

OXFORD
UNIVERSITY PRESS

OXFORD
UNIVERSITY PRESS

Great Clarendon Street, Oxford OX2 6DP,
United Kingdom

Oxford University Press is a department of the University of Oxford.
It furthers the University's objective of excellence in research, scholarship,
and education by publishing worldwide. Oxford is a registered trade mark of
Oxford University Press in the UK and in certain other countries

This collection © Oxford University Press 2003 and 2013

Unless marked otherwise, all pieces (words and music) are by Kathy and David Blackwell and are
© Oxford University Press. All traditional and composed pieces are
arranged by Kathy and David Blackwell and are © Oxford University Press.
Unauthorized arrangement or photocopying of this copyright material is ILLEGAL.

Kathy and David Blackwell have asserted their right under the Copyright,
Designs and Patents Act, 1988, to be identified as the Composers of this Work.

Database right Oxford University Press (maker)

Impression: 11

All rights reserved. No part of this publication may be reproduced,
stored in a retrieval system, or transmitted, in any form or by any means,
without the prior permission in writing of Oxford University Press

Permission to perform the works in this anthology in public
(except in the course of divine worship) should normally be obtained from
a local performing right licensing organization, unless the owner or the occupier
of the premises being used already holds a licence from such an organization.
Likewise, permission to make and exploit a recording of these works
should be obtained from a local mechanical copyright licensing organization

Enquiries concerning reproduction outside the scope of the above
should be directed to the Music Rights Department, Oxford University Press, at
music.permissions.uk@oup.com or at the address above

ISBN 978-0-19-339857-3

Cover illustration by Martin Remphry

Music and text origination by Katie Johnston
Printed in Great Britain on acid-free paper by
Halstan & Co. Ltd, Amersham, Bucks.

Contents

1. Ready to rock 4
2. Clear skies 5
3. Ode to joy (Beethoven) 6
4. Song from the show 7
5. Starry night 8
6. Paris café 9
7. Gaudete! 10
8. Jacob's dance 11
9. Sprint finish 12
10. Bolero 13
11. William Tell (Rossini) 14
12. Country gardens 16
13. You and me 17
14. The road to Donegal 18
15. Full circle 20
16. Thirsty work 21
17. Farewell to Skye 22
18. Lady Katherine's pavane 23
19. Dance of the Sugar Plum Fairy (Tchaikovsky) 24
20. Allegro in A (Telemann) 25
21. Still reeling 26
22. Mexican fiesta 27
23. Show stopper 28
24. Spy movie 30
25. Largo, from the *New World* Symphony (Dvořák) 31
26. Hornpipe, from the *Water Music* (Handel) 32
27. Hungarian folk dance 34
28. Wild West 36
29. Midnight song 38
30. Wade in the water 40
31. Dominant gene 42
32. Chromatic cats 43
33. Show off! 44
34. Little lamb 44
35. Habanera, from *Carmen* (Bizet) 46
36. Alleluia (Boyce) 48
37. Jubilate Deo (Mozart) 48
38. Round Trinidad Bay 48

1. Ready to rock

KB & DB

2. Clear skies

KB & DB

3. Ode to joy

(from Symphony No. 9)

Ludwig van Beethoven (1770–1827)

Also try this in 3rd position using the fingering given.

4. Song from the show

KB & DB

5. Starry night

6. Paris café

KB & DB

7. Gaudete!

Medieval carol

8. Jacob's dance

9. Sprint finish

KB & DB

10. Bolero

Sunny
Spanish trad.
mf
mf
6
f
3
p
f
3
p
11
f
3
p
f
3
p
15
f
cresc.
f
20
rit.
3
3

11. William Tell

G. A. Rossini (1792–1868)

24
ff
p
ff
p
30
cresc.
f
mp
cresc.
f
mp
37
p
p
43
accel. (ad lib.)
cresc.
ff
cresc.
ff

12. Country gardens

English Morris Dance tune

13. You and me

14. The road to Donegal

KB & DB

17
f
p
f
p
21
f
p
f
p
25
f
f
29

15. Full circle

KB & DB

16. Thirsty work

KB & DB

Return to the chorus after each verse. The chorus and verse 1 can be played in semiquavers with spiccato bowing. The music is written out in full in the pupil's book.

17. Farewell to Skye

KB & DB

18. Lady Katherine's pavane

KB & DB

The pavane was a slow, stately court dance popular in the 16th and 17th centuries.

19. Dance of the Sugar Plum Fairy

(from the *Nutcracker* ballet)

P. I. Tchaikovsky (1840–93)

20. Allegro in A

G. P. Telemann (1681–1767)

Try starting this piece with either a down or an up bow.

21. Still reeling

(based on *Blair Atholl*, trad. Scottish reel)

Add your own dynamics to this reel.

22. Mexican fiesta

KB & DB

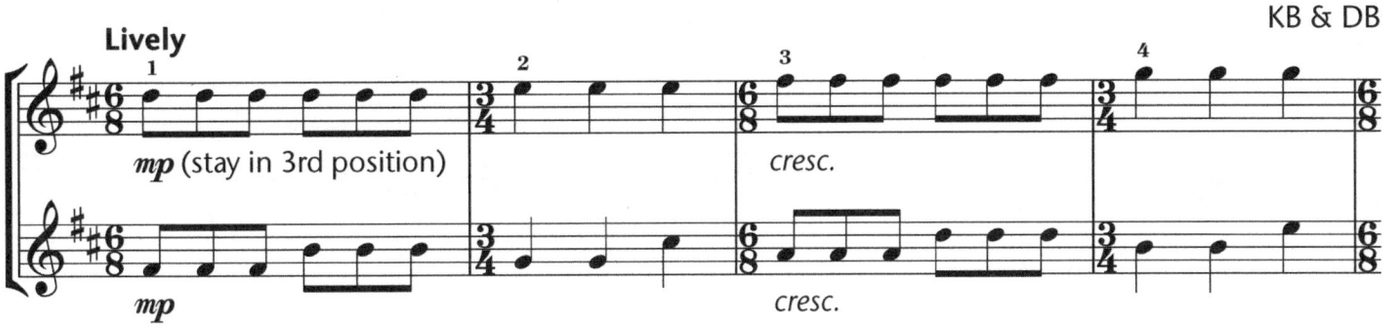

23. Show stopper

23
2
ff
ff
27
f
f
cresc.
ff
ff
31
1
mf
mp
mf
mp
35
cresc.
cresc.
39
mf
cresc.
f
ff
mf
cresc.
f
ff

24. Spy movie

25. Largo

(from the *New World* Symphony)

26. Hornpipe

(from the *Water Music*)

G. F. Handel (1685–1759)

22
4
f
f
25
2
mf
mf
29
mp
mp
f
f
32
3
tr
ff
ff
36
rall.
tr

27. Hungarian folk dance

KB & DB

22
4
27
f
f
32
37
(2nd time **accelerando**)
mf (ff)
p
mf (ff)
sim.
42
1.
2.
ff
ff

28. Wild West

KB & DB

16
cresc.
cresc.
f
f
20
0
1
2
1
1
24
1
28
ff
ff

29. Midnight song

KB & DB

13
mf
cresc.
mf
cresc.
17
mp
mp
21
25
dim.
rall.
dim.
p
p

30. Wade in the water

Spiritual

18
(1
2)
mf
f
mf
22
1
mf
mf
26
0
2
mp
30
Slower
rall.
4
4
1
2
mp
p espress.
p
pp
freely

31. Dominant gene

KB & DB

32. Chromatic cats

KB & DB

33. Show off!

KB & DB

34. Little lamb

Spiritual

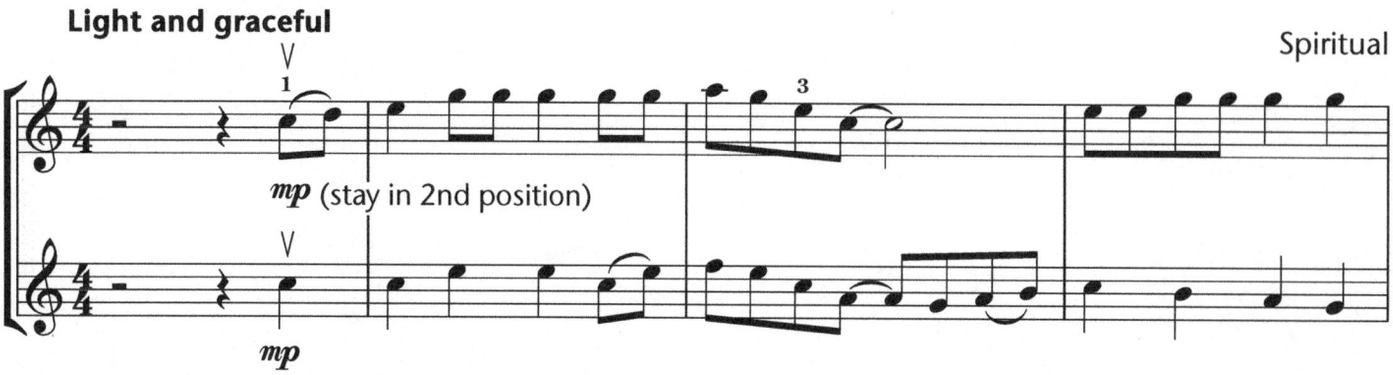

5
4
10
3
f
mp
f
f
mp
f
15
3
mp
mp
20
4
25
rall.
0
2
mp
dim.
p
mp
dim.
p

35. Habanera

(from *Carmen*)

Georges Bizet (1838–75)

18
mf
sim.
arco
mf
sim.
22
26
1
f
2
f
31
1
3
con rubato
4
3
ff
ff

Round up

Play these rounds or canons in 2 or more parts, entering at *.

36. Alleluia

William Boyce (1711–79)

37. Jubilate Deo

W. A. Mozart (1756–91)

38. Round Trinidad Bay

KB & DB